Regulating Low-Skilled
Immigration in the United States

Regulating Low-Skilled Immigration in the United States

Gordon H. Hanson

Distributed by arrangement with the Rowman & Littlefield Publishing Group, 4501 Forbes Boulevard, Suite 200, Lanham, Maryland 20706. To order call toll free 1-800-462-6420 or 1-717-794-3800. For all other inquiries please contact AEI Press, 1150 Seventeenth Street, N.W., Washington, D.C. 20036 or call 1-800-862-5801.

NRI NATIONAL
RESEARCH
INITIATIVE

This publication is a project of the National Research Initiative, a program of the American Enterprise Institute that is designed to support, publish, and disseminate research by university-based scholars and other independent researchers who are engaged in the exploration of important public policy issues.

Library of Congress Cataloging-in-Publication Data

Hanson, Gordon.
  Regulating low-skilled immigration in the United States / Gordon
Hanson.
      p. cm.
  ISBN-13: 978-0-8447-4370-7 (pbk. : alk. paper)
  ISBN-10: 0-8447-4370-4 (pbk. : alk. paper)
  ISBN-13: 978-0-8447-4371-4 (ebook : alk. paper)
  ISBN-10: 0-8447-4371-2 (ebook : alk. paper)
  1. Foreign workers—Government policy--United States. 2. Unskilled
labor—United States. 3. United States—Emigration and immigration. I.
Title.
  HD8081.A5.H36 2010
  325.73—dc22

                                                        2010023098

Printed in the United States of America

Contents

List of Figures

Introduction

In 2007, the U.S. Congress came close to voting on a major reform of immigration laws. The various legislative proposals under consideration all shared an emphasis on strengthening border security, expanding the number of visas for foreign guest workers, and defining a path to legal residence for illegal immigrants living in the country. Illegal immigration was, of course, the motivation for the proposed overhaul. With 11.9 million undocumented residents in the United States (see figure I-1), there is widespread agreement that the current immigration system is broken, having failed the basic test of controlling national borders. The Obama administration is likely to push Congress to address immigration before 2012, given that illegal entry continues to account for nearly half of the low-skilled foreign workers in the United States.[1] Whether change will occur through significant new legislation or incremental reforms is unclear. As large numbers of immigrants continue to enter the country illegally every year, what is certain is that the issue will not be resolved any time soon.

The recession that began in late 2007 has taken immediate pressure off of Congress to create a new immigration framework. The Pew Hispanic Center estimates that the number of illegal immigrants in the U.S. labor force fell modestly from 8.5 million in 2007 to 8.3 million in 2008, after a decade and a half of steady growth (Passel and Cohn 2009a). The decline reflects the recent collapse of U.S. labor demand, which began in the housing sector and then spread to the rest of the economy. In 2007, the share of undocumented workers employed in construction reached 18 percent, making it the country's largest source of jobs for illegal laborers. Manufacturing, retail trade, and agriculture are the next most important sectors. As work in construction and other labor-intensive industries has precipitously declined, some immigrants have returned to their native countries (Passel and Cohn 2009b).

1

FIGURE I-1
U.S. POPULATION OF UNAUTHORIZED IMMIGRANTS, 1980–2009

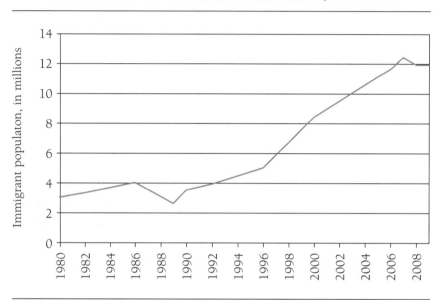

SOURCE: Passel and Cohn (2009a).

Though net inflows of undocumented entrants have dropped, gross inflows have remained at high levels. Net inflow is the difference between the number of illegal immigrants who enter the country and the number who depart; gross inflow is simply the number who enter. Researchers know that gross inflows continue to be significant because the U.S. Border Patrol continues to apprehend large numbers of individuals attempting to enter the country illegally. Nationwide, the Border Patrol captured 742,000 "deportable aliens" in 2008, down from 847,000 in 2007 (see figure I-2).[2] Although these statistics signal a slight decrease in illegal entry, the 2008 data indicate that gross inflows of the undocumented remain large. When the economy—and the construction industry in particular—begins to recover, so will net inflows of unauthorized immigrants, renewing pressure on Congress to act.

The intent of the 2007 round of proposed reforms was to convert illegal immigrants into legal immigrants. The transformation would have been

FIGURE I-2

APPREHENSIONS OF ILLEGAL IMMIGRANTS BY U.S. BORDER PATROL,
1987–2008

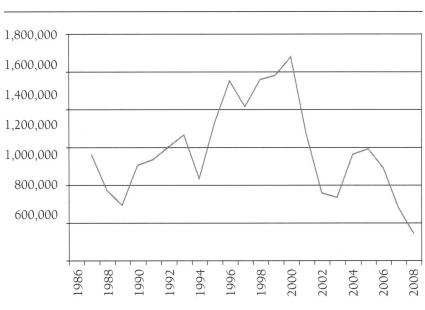

SOURCE: U.S. Department of Homeland Security (2009).

accomplished by deterring future unauthorized entry (through enforcement), increasing legal options for low-skilled work in the United States
(through temporary work visas), and legalizing the existing population of
undocumented immigrants (through an amnesty of some kind). Though
lawmakers disagree about the size of the role each mechanism should play,
the mechanisms themselves have been subject to less scrutiny. Yet, successful immigration reform depends on getting the mechanisms right. Illegal
immigration is, in large part, a response to market signals that encourage
individuals to move from low-wage labor markets in Mexico, Central
America, and elsewhere to the United States. Efforts to curtail illegal entry
will fail unless Congress builds a system that is responsive to these signals.

Historically, there has been a correlation between high levels of illegal
immigration and economic growth. During the U.S. economic expansion
between 2002 and 2007, unauthorized migrants entered the country in large

numbers, particularly at the peak of the U.S. housing boom. Likewise, in the 1990s, when the United States enjoyed rapid growth, and Mexico suffered a financial crisis, illegal entry was also at high levels (Hanson and Spilimbergo 1999). Once in the country, undocumented migrants are geographically mobile, moving among states in response to regional business cycles. Today, unauthorized immigrants have a significant presence in most parts of the United States and have become an integral part of the low-skilled labor force. According to 2006 statistics, they account for 20 percent of working-age adults in the United States with less than a high school education.[3]

If implemented, the 2007 immigration reforms would have radically altered how the United States governs low-skilled immigration. In concert with strict border enforcement, most low-skilled immigrants would have been required to obtain a temporary work visa granting the right to work for a particular U.S. employer for a specified period of time. Switching employers or extending residence in the United States would have required official approval. The U.S. government, in effect, would have replaced the market as the entity managing the flow of low-skilled labor into the country and between employers.

When the Obama administration revisits the issue of immigration reform, should it pick up where Congress left off in 2007? Is the current U.S. framework for legal immigration the right model for incorporating existing illegal immigrants into the labor force? Would increasing existing temporary worker programs be an effective way to govern the immigration of low-skilled workers? The policy debate has focused much more on what the American public dislikes about illegal immigration—the primary complaint being, simply, that it is illegal[4]—than on whether the country would be well served by the legal options under consideration.

In this monograph, I compare the United States' current system for governing low-skilled immigration with new mechanisms that Congress might consider under future reform proposals. My goal is to explain the logic behind illegal immigration and place this logic in the context of various means of managing a low-skilled foreign labor force. Low-skilled immigration raises U.S. national income by making domestic capital more productive, even after accounting for income losses suffered by low-skilled native workers (Borjas 1999). However, increasing the number of low-skilled residents in the country may increase the net tax burden on native taxpayers. Ensuring that low-skilled immigration makes the United States generally better off requires a system that attracts individuals with a strong attachment to the U.S. labor force who do not place excessive demands on public services. Moreover, the supply of these immigrants must be sensitive to economic conditions.

Illegal immigration, as regulated by market forces, largely satisfies these criteria—but at the cost of undermining the rule of law and creating a population with limited legal protection and restricted options for assimilating into mainstream society. To construct a better system for managing low-skilled immigration, Congress should preserve the features of the current regime that serve the country well and strip away the features that are corrosive to civil society and harmful to immigrants.

In chapter 1 of this monograph, I present a framework for classifying immigration regimes. When the government designs an admission policy, it makes choices regarding three regulatory features (Hanson 2010). The first is whether to manage immigration inflows using prices or quantities. The level of U.S. legal immigration is determined by the number of permanent and temporary admission visas currently available; this method regulates the system quantity. The United States manages illegal immigration through border enforcement, which determines the cost of entry and regulates the system price.[5] Whether a country uses quantities or prices to regulate immigration affects the qualities of the individuals who enter. A price mechanism generally does a better job of attracting immigrants who place a high value on being able to work in the United States and are, therefore, highly productive; a quantity mechanism only works as well as the rationing principle it uses to allocate visas to applicants in the queue.

Whether entrants are admitted based on an *ex ante* or *ex post* screening mechanism is the second feature of policy concern for immigration regimes. Most legal immigrants obtain a visa either through a relative in the United States or through sponsorship by a U.S. employer.[6] The family status or professional qualifications of an individual determine whether he or she will qualify for entry, meaning that legal entrants are subject to an *ex ante* screen—eligibility for permanent residency is based on observable characteristics at the time of entry. Legal immigrants lose the right of residence only if they break U.S. laws or return to their home country for an extended period of time.

Illegal immigrants, on the other hand, acquire the *de facto* right to remain in the United States by finding work and staying out of trouble. Since it is their behavior after entry that determines their immigration status, they are subject to an *ex post* screen. A tradeoff exists between the *ex ante* and *ex post* screening mechanisms; the former provides stronger incentives to assimilate, and the latter provides stronger incentives to work hard and be economically productive.

The third feature of immigration regimes is the scope of residency rights. Legal immigrants holding green cards have broad residency rights, including the option to remain in the country indefinitely and to apply for citizenship three to five years after obtaining the visa. Once an individual has a green card, the burden to obtain citizenship is low. For illegal immigrants, however, residency rights are rather narrow, consisting of the rights to fire and police protection, emergency medical attention, and public schooling, but not most other public services. Undocumented entrants lack any guarantee of being allowed to remain in the United States beyond the uncertain prospect of future amnesty. There are also tradeoffs in the scope of residency rights; broader rights encourage immigrants to make investments that strengthen their ties to the United States, while narrower rights limit the fiscal exposure of U.S. taxpayers to illegal immigration.

In chapter 2 of this monograph, I examine how the current U.S. immigration regime affects the composition of legal and illegal immigrants and how this composition would change if the United States adopted alternative mechanisms to govern the inflow of low-skilled foreign labor. I focus less on the technical details regarding reform and more on providing an analytical framework to evaluate the choices Congress faces in designing a new regime for managing low-skilled immigration.[7]

One central challenge in constructing immigration policy is determining how to select the "right" individuals for entry. Given the large income differences between the United States and the rest of the world, there is an excess demand for U.S. immigration visas in the world economy. The criteria for selecting visa recipients include: family ties to U.S. residents (which affect the well-being of U.S. residents); desired skills or professional qualifications (which affect U.S. productivity); or emigration from a country undergoing a humanitarian crisis (which affects U.S. cultural sensibilities and foreign policy objectives). Changing the immigration regime would modify the composition of entrants and alter the overall impact of immigration on the United States, even if the level of immigration remained constant.

The 2007 reforms would have attempted to replace the current regime of illegal immigration—which is subject to price regulation, an *ex post* screening mechanism, and narrow residency rights—with an expanded temporary work program. While the details regarding temporary workers were not fully delineated in the 2007 reforms, the proposed mechanisms involved quantity regulation (fixing the number of visas extended to entrants), an *ex ante* screening mechanism (selecting entrants based on their applications), and moderate residency rights (allowing temporary visa holders to renew their visas and ultimately seek legal permanent residence).

But such reforms would not necessarily maximize the benefit of immigration to the U.S. economy. Under the current system, immigrants who enter the country illegally have strong incentives to stay employed, work hard, and avoid criminal activity. The current regime also allows for flexible levels of immigration that vary according to business-cycle conditions in the United States. Once in the United States, illegal immigrants have an incentive to move among U.S. regions in response to variations in regional labor demand. A temporary or provisional worker program, unless properly designed, will lack many of these attractive properties.

In chapter 3 of this monograph, I examine the effects of immigration on the U.S. economy and outline the broad principles Congress should follow in regulating the entry of low-skilled foreign labor. U.S. policy goals include raising U.S. gross domestic product (GDP); transforming illegal entrants into legal entrants; attracting workers who are unlikely to be a fiscal burden; allowing immigration levels to be responsive to U.S. economic conditions; and containing the cost of enforcement of illegal immigration. An efficient regime for achieving these goals would allocate visas through a price mechanism, use a combination of *ex ante* and *ex post* screening mechanisms in admitting immigrants, and offer a graduated system of residency rights.

Even under a regime that utilizes these mechanisms efficiently, illegal immigration cannot be eliminated entirely. For numerous sectors of the U.S. economy, the cost of preventing the employment of illegal immigrants exceeds any conceivable benefit. The goal of immigration reform should not be to reduce illegal immigration to zero, as such reduction is not cost-effective. However, it is possible and economically advantageous to reduce illegal immigration by a large measure.

The regime I describe differs markedly from that considered by Congress in 2007. Arguably, the 2007 reforms would have been worse for the United States than simply leaving intact the current regime of illegal immigration.

1

Immigration Policy Regimes: The United States in International Perspective

Why do the United States and other developed nations restrict immigration? One simple answer is that inflows of foreign labor change the distribution of income, which causes political conflict over immigration policy and, in turn, creates opposing demands on the management of borders. How a society resolves these conflicts and demands determines how many and what type of immigrants are admitted, and the rights and privileges they enjoy.

The Political Economy of Immigration

From a global perspective, international migration offers clear economic benefits. Consider the gain from emigration for a typical worker in Mexico, whom for measurement purposes I will take to be a thirty-five-year-old urban male with nine years of education, making him slightly older and somewhat more educated than the average worker in that country (Hanson 2006). Simply by moving from Mexico to the United States, our typical worker's annual income would increase by 250 percent, even after controlling for cost-of-living differences between the two countries (Clemons, Montenegro, and Pritchett 2008). The income gain from migration is largely a result of international differences in labor productivity. Labor in Mexico is less productive than in the United States because Mexico's employers use less capital per worker, employ inferior technology, rely on a poorer infrastructure, and are supported by a weaker institutional environment, among other factors. Migration reallocates labor from where it is less productive to where it is more productive, raising global income in the process. What is there for the United States not to like?

To understand U.S. policy choices, the relevant question is not whether immigration makes the United States as a whole better off, but whether the interest groups that typically benefit from immigration are more influential than those that suffer. Because immigration changes the labor supply, it affects the distribution of income. Low-skilled immigration raises the supply of less-skilled labor, which, all else remaining equal, tends to put downward pressure on the wages of low-skilled workers. This wage pressure may account for why increases in low-skilled immigration tend to reduce the price of non-traded domestic services for U.S. households (Cortes 2008).

There is active debate among labor economists over the wage impacts of immigration. Some find that labor inflows have hurt low-skilled natives (for example, Borjas 2003), and others discover effects that are very small (for example, Card 2005). Whatever the true impact may be, politicians are motivated by the impact that voters perceive. Surveys of voter preferences on immigration policy suggest that low-skilled individuals—whether classified by education, income, or occupation—are the group most opposed to easing restrictions on immigration (Scheve and Slaughter 2001; Hanson, Scheve, and Slaughter 2007). Lobbying by labor unions and other groups representing low-skilled workers exerts pressure on Congress to restrict labor inflows from abroad.

But the preferences of low-skilled workers cannot be the whole story. The labor market segment most affected by low-skilled immigration—native-born workers with less than a high school education—accounts for just 8 percent of the native labor force (Borjas 2003). Furthermore, in recent years, labor unions, which had long been opposed to immigration, have become more accommodating of foreign labor (though not of illegal immigration or guest-worker programs), now that first- or second-generation immigrants account for much of their growth in membership (Briggs 2001).

Taxpayers are another important bloc opposed to immigration. If low-skilled immigrants receive more in public benefits than they pay in taxes, their presence in the country increases the fiscal burden on natives, who, as a consequence, face higher taxes, benefit from fewer public services, and experience more public-sector borrowing. These effects are felt most acutely in high-immigration regions, owing to the fact that much of the income and payroll tax revenues generated by immigrants accrue to the federal government, while the fiscal cost of paying for the public education and health care services used by immigrants falls primarily on states and localities.

Fiscal conservatives have considerable political weight in the United States, given their prominence in the Republican Party. Their opposition to immigration in 2007 helped derail attempts to legalize unauthorized immigrants and expand visas for guest workers. Out of concern about offending the party's conservative base, Republican presidential candidate John McCain, who previously had been a leading advocate for immigration reform, gave the issue little attention in his 2008 campaign. Results from individual surveys show that U.S. residents who are more exposed to fiscal pressures from immigration—primarily those living in states with large immigrant populations that provide immigrants access to generous public benefits—are more in favor of reducing immigration.

The public finance divide over immigration is strongest among natives with high earnings potential, who tend to be in higher tax brackets (Hanson, Scheve, and Slaughter 2007). For instance, high-income earners in low-tax Texas tend to be less opposed to immigration than high-income earners in high-tax California, a feature reflected in the mid-1990s gubernatorial campaign strategies of George W. Bush and Pete Wilson. Both were anti-tax, pro–free trade Republicans, but the Texan Bush was largely supportive of immigration, while the Californian Wilson staked his political career on its opposition (Hanson 2005).

Interest groups that *favor* immigration include businesses that hire foreign workers. Recent research on how foreign guest workers are allocated across industries finds that industries that spend more on lobbying the government on immigration issues, including many high-tech businesses, succeed in obtaining a larger number of guest worker visas (Facchini, Mayda, and Mishra 2008). These lobbying activities provide evidence that immigration benefits employers, consistent with standard economic theory that inflows of labor raise the marginal product of capital. Because immigration is good for business, business pushes Congress to keep U.S. borders open.

Other evidence of business pressure in favor of immigration emerges in the ways in which the U.S. government manages illegal immigration. In 2005, the Western Growers Association, a business lobby representing farmers in the western states, complained to Washington that excessive

border enforcement was preventing farmers in Arizona from hiring suffi-
cient labor to harvest their winter lettuce crop.[1] In 1998, raids by immigration authorities in Georgia onion fields prompted the U.S. Attorney General,
both U.S. senators from Georgia, and three Georgia congressional repre-
sentatives to criticize the federal government for injuring Georgia farmers.[2]
In the 1940s and 1950s, the district commissioner of the U.S. Border Patrol
routinely issued orders to stop apprehending illegal immigrants during the
agricultural harvest season (Calavita 1992).

These examples suggest that business pressure makes border enforcement sensitive to changes in economic conditions for industries that typically hire undocumented workers. In theory, higher relative prices of goods
produced by immigrant-intensive industries would increase the returns of
lobbying against border enforcement. Statistical evidence supports this link;
controlling for macroeconomic conditions, an increase in the relative price
of goods for an immigrant-intensive industry today is associated with a
decrease in border enforcement six to ten months in the future (Hanson and
Spilimbergo 2001). This association suggests that authorities relax enforcement when the demand for undocumented workers rises.

In sum, the impact of immigration on the distribution of income
induces special interest groups to lobby the government on immigration
policy. Business groups tend to favor freer immigration and thus lobby to
keep barriers low. Labor groups and taxpayers tend to oppose immigration
and lobby to keep barriers high. In addressing low-skilled immigration,
Congress has accommodated these conflicting pressures by maintaining
high and rigid barriers to legal inflows (relative to the number of individuals
worldwide who seek a U.S. green card) and porous and flexible barriers to
illegal inflows.

The Design of Immigration Policy Regimes

The opposition of taxpayers to the arrival of foreign labor reveals a tension
between free immigration and the maintenance of the welfare state, as
famously recognized by Milton Friedman.[3] Any government that provides
means-tested entitlements puts its public finances at risk by allowing the
immigration of individuals who qualify for benefits. Because most rich

countries provide entitlements, their governments have created mechanisms to prevent low-skilled immigration from undermining the welfare system.

Temporary Worker Programs. One solution is to deny welfare benefits to low-skilled immigrants, which allows the receiving country to gain the productive labor of illegal immigrants without increasing the fiscal burden on native taxpayers. Temporary worker programs serve this purpose. They grant foreign workers admission to the receiving country, but only under restricted residency rights that limit their stay in the country and their access to public services. Yet, in most advanced countries, guest-worker programs remain small. In 2005, the total number of temporary immigrant workers, including individuals at all skill levels, comprised just 3 percent of immigrants in the United States (Camarota 2005). Most guest workers are high-skilled; the H-1B visa program, which admits 65,000 workers per year for three-year stays, is the largest gateway for temporary immigration in the United States (U.S. Department of Homeland Security 2009). In European countries, temporary immigrants are also a small share of total immigration.

Most temporary low-skilled legal immigration in the United States occurs under the H-2A (seasonal agricultural worker) or H-2B (seasonal non-agricultural worker) visa programs, which permit visa holders to work for a particular U.S. employer for up to a 364-day period and are renewable twice (U.S. Department of Homeland Security 2009). H-2B visas are capped at 66,000 per year; H-2A visas have no cap but are subject to onerous requirements and strict work rules that limit their use.[4] In most years, H-2B visa admissions are comparable to or exceed H-2A visa admissions. Since H-2 visa holders are required to leave the United States at the end of their employment, the number of annual entrants represents the total population of temporary legal workers in the country. Compared to the roughly 8.3 million illegal immigrants employed in the United States, temporary low-skilled legal immigrants (who total less than 150,000 individuals at any point in time) are an inconsequential component of the low-skilled U.S. labor force (Passel and Cohn 2009a).

Guest workers account for a large fraction of low-skilled immigration in non-democratic countries, including the Gulf States, Hong Kong, and Singapore (Rupert 1999; Winckler 1999). In 2000, the largest labor-importing countries in the Middle East—Bahrain, Jordan, Kuwait, Qatar, Saudi Arabia, and the United Arab Emirates—were the destinations for 6.4 percent of the world's international migrants. Most low-skilled immigrants in the Gulf States come from poor countries in Asia and the Middle East; Bangladesh, Egypt, India, Indonesia, Pakistan, the Philippines, and Yemen are the primary source countries of the Gulf States' foreign labor.

Why would the Gulf States be willing to admit large numbers of low-skilled immigrants as guest workers while the United States and Europe effectively force similar labor inflows to be illegal? One explanation is that non-democratic countries are better able to enforce the departure provisions of guest worker contracts (Massey 2004). The Gulf States tend to be aggressive in deporting illegal immigrants; they further restrict undocumented entry by limiting contact between temporary immigrants and the host population, and back-loading labor compensation until an immigrant returns home (Shah 2006). Enforcing departure requires immigration authorities to monitor the movements of immigrants, as a government cannot deport immigrants who violate the terms of their visas unless it can locate them. Monitoring may be aided by the internal surveillance that non-democratic countries maintain as part of their national security infrastructure. Tight internal security may make it difficult for illegal immigrants to evade apprehension, suggesting that the watchful eye of the state enhances the capability of governments to manage large-scale temporary immigration.

In the United States, there is intense resistance to government surveillance of individual activities. Protection of civil liberties, therefore, complicates the internal enforcement of temporary immigration visas (Martin 2001), as authorities are limited in the methods they can use to obtain information about where immigrants live and work. If immigrants choose to overstay their visas or violate the terms of their temporary labor contracts, there is often little the U.S. government can do to stop them (Passel and Cohn 2009a), other than denying them admission in the first place.

One consequence of imperfect vigilance may be that voters are skeptical about the ability of the U.S. government to ensure that temporary migrants return home after their labor contracts are completed. Weak enforcement of the departure provisions for low-skilled foreign guest workers may lead voters to view such programs as "open-ended" immigration. This perception may undermine political support of low-skilled immigration in general (Briggs 2004).

Origins of Illegal Immigration. Another way to resolve the conflict between immigration and the welfare state is to allow most low-skilled foreign workers no other option but to enter the country illegally. Illegal immigration provides the receiving country with access to the labor it desires while limiting the fiscal consequences of labor inflows. Illegal immigrants now account for 30 percent of the U.S. foreign-born population (Passel and Cohn 2009a). In the European Union, the gross annual inflow of illegal immigrants is 650,000 to 800,000 individuals per year (Jandl 2003), a level comparable to the U.S. gross inflow.[5]

The U.S. government devotes considerable resources to enforcing national borders against illegal immigration, but simple observation suggests that these efforts are not very effective. Between 1992 and 2008, total hours worked by U.S. Border Patrol officers increased by a factor of four (see figure 1-1). In fiscal year 2009, the United States allocated $18 billion in spending on border- and transportation-security activities, up from $16 billion in 2008.[6] Enforcement against illegal immigration constitutes much of this expenditure. In 2009, the budgets for Customs and Border Protection (which oversees border enforcement) and Immigration and Customs Enforcement (which oversees interior enforcement) were $9.5 billion and $5.4 billion, respectively.[7] Over the ten-year period from 1999 through 2008, enforcement by U.S. immigration authorities resulted in an average annual apprehension of 1.1 million individuals who had been attempting to enter the country illegally along the southwestern border. Despite these efforts, the illegal population rose by a net 500,000 individuals per year during the same period (Passel and Cohn 2009a). The federal government could have spent more on border enforcement but chose not to; high levels of illegal immigration, therefore, reflect a tacit decision by the U.S. government to allow illegal entry. Illegal immigration is a policy choice, albeit an implicit one.

To understand why the United States permits both legal immigration and illegal immigration, it is helpful to review the mechanisms that countries use to govern both kind of admission.

Regulating Legal Immigration. The U.S. government regulates legal immigration through a combination of numerical quotas, entry-selection criteria, and restrictions on residency rights. While many countries have

FIGURE 1-1

U.S. BORDER PATROL OFFICER HOURS, SOUTHWEST SECTORS, 1992–2008

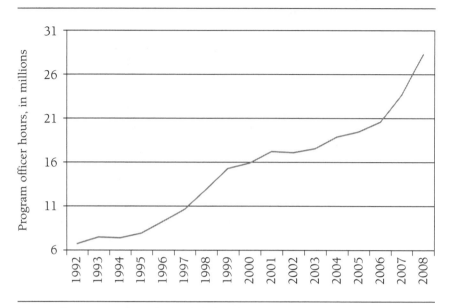

SOURCE: US Department of Homeland Security (2009).

admission categories that allow unrestricted immigration, these are generally limited to immediate family members of citizens, as in the United States,
or individuals from countries within an economic bloc, as in the European
Union. Other legal immigrants are subject to quotas; quotas vary according
to a nation's *ex ante* selection criteria. The United States allocates the majority of permanent residence visas to relatives of U.S. citizens and legal residents. Australia and Canada favor legal immigrants who meet designated
skill criteria, while many European countries reserve a large share of visas
for refugees and asylees (OECD 2008).

U.S. visas come with specified residency rights. Temporary visas set a
time limit for residence (for example, less than one year with two possible
renewals for low-skilled guest workers on H-2A or H-2B visas; and three
years, renewable once, for high-skilled guest workers on H-1B visas[8]); the
types of jobs a visa holder may obtain (U.S. temporary workers are
required to work for the employer who originally sponsored them, unless
they find a new employer willing to sponsor them); and the set of

government benefits to which the visa holder has access (non-citizens are excluded from most federally funded entitlement programs) (U.S. Department of Homeland Security 2009). A permanent visa in the form of a green card provides broader residency rights, including mobility between employers and a defined path to citizenship, as visa holders become eligible to naturalize after five years (or three years, in the case of individuals married to U.S. citizens).

Regulating Illegal Immigration. The U.S. government regulates illegal immigration in multiple ways: through border enforcement, which affects ease of entry; through interior enforcement, which helps determine who can stay; and through laws that define residency rights. By choosing the intensity with which the Border Patrol polices national borders, the government, in theory, influences the smuggling fee that illegal immigrants pay a *coyote* to help them enter the United States (Ethier 1986). The charge is the effective cost that migrants incur to gain access to the U.S. labor market. When border enforcement rises, it becomes more dangerous for *coyotes* to smuggle migrants, causing them to raise their fees (Gathmann 2008). For migrants who choose to cross the border without the aid of a *coyote,* the intensity of border enforcement affects the amount of time and energy they expend and the risks they incur, setting an implicit entry cost.

The smuggling cost is understood as an upfront investment that migrants make in order to earn a return in the form of high U.S. wages. For our typical Mexican worker, the return is a 250 percent increase in income, amounting to a gross income gain of approximately $10,000 (Hanson 2009). When the smuggling cost rises, the return that immigrants must earn to justify their upfront investment also increases. Individuals earning adequate salaries in their home countries may choose not to migrate when stronger border enforcement causes smuggling fees to increase. Empirically, stronger border enforcement tends to reduce the probability of migrating to the United States for individuals in Mexico; the decline is greatest for less-educated workers (Orrenius and Zavodny 2005). Stronger border enforcement thus reduces immigration overall and shifts the composition of immigration toward those with higher education levels.

Ex post selection criteria depend on U.S. interior enforcement policies. Individuals who are able to thwart capture by evading both immigration authorities and the police earn the *de facto* right to stay in the country (Cox and Posner 2007). Until 2006, the United States concentrated enforcement on the border rather than in the interior, allowing most illegal immigrants who did not commit crimes or assume high public profiles to remain on U.S. soil (Orrenius and Zavodny 2010). For illegal immigrants, the penalty for committing a crime is not just the possibility of jail time, it is deportation (as well as a temporary or permanent ban on being able to obtain a green card). Non-citizens convicted of a felony that carries a sentence of one year or more are automatically deported upon completion of their prison term. Those who commit lesser crimes also face deportation if police turn them over to immigration authorities. Perhaps as a consequence of the high penalties for criminal behavior, immigrants are much less likely than natives with similar age and education profiles to be incarcerated, suggesting a lower inclination to engage in crime (Butcher and Piehl 2006).

Toward the end of his second term, President George W. Bush changed U.S. policies on interior enforcement. Beginning in late 2006, U.S. immigration authorities dramatically increased large-scale raids of U.S. worksites and sought to locate immigrants who had ignored deportation orders (Camarota 2008). The government incorporated local law enforcement officers into the interior enforcement effort by applying section 287(g) of the Immigration and Nationality Act (added to the law by the Illegal Immigration Reform and Immigrant Responsibility Act in 1996), which grants officers the authority to check an individual's immigration status during traffic stops or other routine encounters.

The U.S. government has increased interior enforcement against illegal immigration at several points in the past (the early 1950s, 1987, 1994, and 2001), only to relax these efforts once economic conditions generated an increase in the demand for labor (Hanson 2006). The Obama administration has weakened some of the Bush administration's enforcement policies by no longer seeking to prosecute illegal immigrants for identity theft and shifting the focus of interior enforcement from workers to employers. But the current administration has maintained and expanded other provisions, including employer audits, the E-Verify program for electronically checking worker employment eligibility, and coordination between the federal government and local law enforcement under 287(g).

Although illegal immigrants lack official residency rights and, therefore, are always at risk for deportation, they are not devoid of legal protections. Illegal immigrants may report crimes, attend public schools, seek emergency medical services, obtain bank loans, and even acquire a driver's license (in some states), with minimal risk of deportation. Minimum-wage laws apply to illegal immigrants, though the incentive of undocumented workers to seek enforcement of such provisions may be weakened by fear of exposure to immigration authorities. Children born in the United States are eligible for all public benefits accorded to U.S. citizens and are themselves eligible for citizenship at birth.[9] What illegal immigrants lack is a defined path to legal permanent residence. While future immigration reform may include an amnesty provision, the last legislative act granting a broad amnesty was passed in 1986, suggesting that legalization is an uncertain and infrequent outcome for illegal immigrants.

Immigrant Selection and Immigration Regimes

The United States manages legal immigration by regulating the quantity of visas, screening immigrants at entry, and providing broad residency rights, but manages illegal immigration by affecting entry prices, screening migrant behavior after entry, and providing narrow residency rights. What does the United States achieve by maintaining separate policy regimes for legal and illegal immigration?

Selection of Legal Immigrants. In legal immigration, quantity regulation allows the United States to achieve specific goals in admissions by assigning quotas to particular categories of individuals. The allocation of quotas may reflect a desire to maximize the immigration surplus (by admitting scarce labor types), political economy constraints on the level and type of immigrant inflows, or other objectives of government (for example, national security, cultural homogeneity, or humanitarian concerns).

The cost of this *ex ante* screening of legal immigrants is that the government forgoes the option to obtain information about an immigrant beyond observable characteristics before offering admission (Cox and Posner 2007). However, the cost of undiscovered information may be small for skilled immigrants whose abilities are verifiable in the form of educational degrees, professional awards, and past employment. The information cost may also be small in countries that possess strong preferences for specific types of entrants (for example, family members of current citizens). In these cases, any *ex post* information on immigrant behavior may not alter the admission decision.

Combining an *ex ante* screen with broad residency rights may give immigrants a strong incentive to assimilate. By reducing uncertainty over an individual's eligibility to remain in the United States, broad residency rights encourage immigrants to make both monetary and social investments in their new communities, such as buying homes, joining community organizations, or acquiring occupation-specific training. All of these activities create long-term payoffs for U.S. society. However, broad residency rights also carry a high fiscal cost because they give immigrants access to full government benefits after citizenship. The cost of providing broad rights may be small for skilled immigrants, whose income-earning ability makes them net contributors to government coffers. But for low-skilled immigrants, the fiscal cost of admission is far higher (Hanson 2005).

Quotas do not result in as much inflexibility in immigration levels as it would seem, since countries often admit a mix of permanent and temporary entrants. Opponents to immigration are often unwilling to support permanent status for all entrants. Temporary immigration quotas give politicians the power to rescind visas in the future, a provision that may increase support for immigration. Comparing the costs and benefits of this system, we might expect the share of legally admitted temporary immigrants to be higher when an economy is closer to a business-cycle peak, at which point the option value of being able to expel temporary immigrants in the future may be relatively high.

The United States follows this pattern to a rough extent; the number of H-1B visas for high-skilled workers allocated annually rose from 65,000 to 195,000 during the late 1990s economic boom and fell during the recession of 2001 and 2002. However, the time-series correlation between temporary visas and the business cycle is weak. In general, the level of legal immigration is unresponsive to economic conditions (Hanson 2007).

Constitutional rules governing citizenship are another factor that constrain legal immigration policy regimes. Countries typically allow individuals to acquire citizenship by birth, naturalization, or marriage. Under the *jus soli* principle, which is rooted in both civil and common-law traditions, citizenship is acquired by place of birth, implying that the native-born child of an immigrant is a citizen. Under the *jus sanguinis* principle, citizenship is acquired by descent, such that the child of a citizen is also a citizen, regardless of birthplace. Current citizenship laws often embody both principles, though they tend to have emerged out of one tradition or the other.

Jus soli was predominant in Europe through the eighteenth century, given feudal traditions linking citizenship to land. The French adopted *jus sanguinis* in the early nineteenth century; the tradition then spread throughout continental Europe and its colonies. The United Kingdom, however, preserved *jus soli,* which was eventually adopted by the United States, Canada, and Australia (Bertocchi and Strozzi 2006). Under a *jus sanguinis* tradition, a country may have difficulty in granting broad residency rights to immigrants whose parents were not citizens. The United States utilizes a mix of *jus soli* and *jus sanguinis,* as children of immigrants born in the country are citizens, as well as children born to U.S. citizens residing abroad. Because children of illegal immigrants qualify for U.S. citizenship, their parents may feel a connection to the United States that is stronger than their own immigrant status would suggest. This connection may complicate political decisions over the fate of illegal immigrants.

Source-country policies may also affect whether immigrants become naturalized in destination countries. During the 1990s, Brazil, Colombia, Costa Rica, the Dominican Republic, and Ecuador each enacted laws permitting dual citizenship. Between 1990 and 2000, U.S. naturalization rates for eligible immigrants from these countries increased relative to immigrants from other countries. That is, once they could hold dual citizenship, individuals from these countries began to naturalize in the United States in larger numbers. Thus, it appears that not having to give up citizenship in their source countries speeds immigrants' assimilation in their destination countries (Mazzolari 2009).

Selection of Illegal Immigrants. For illegal immigration, entry prices and selection criteria are implicitly defined by the intensity of border and interior enforcement (Ethier 1986). Entry prices serve as a selection device, since an individual must value migration enough to be willing to incur the cost of paying a smuggler. Entry fees thus select immigrants with relatively large perceived income gains (Orrenius and Zavodny 2005), including those for whom immigration would yield large gains in either pre-tax income (due to a productivity gain from immigration) or post-tax income (due to tax and transfer policies in the destination country). While most destination countries would prefer to attract the first type of immigrant over the second, an entry price does not select between the two.

Granting narrow residency rights is one way to encourage immigration of more productive illegal immigrants. Since 1996, non-citizens in the United States have been ineligible for most types of federally funded public assistance (Fix and Passel 2002). A second way to encourage productive illegal immigrants is through *ex post* screening. Interior enforcement helps screen out illegal immigrants who commit crimes, try to obtain government benefits illicitly, or engage in other behavior deemed objectionable. Governments that choose *not* to monitor employers that hire illegal immigrants can ensure that illegal immigrants who come to work are able to remain in the country.

The combination of price regulation, narrow residency rights, and *ex post* screening helps countries attract productive and motivated illegal immigrants. This selection process may be particularly important for low-skilled workers, whose observable characteristics do not provide a qualifiable demonstration of their productivity. In the United States, two-thirds of immigrants with less than a high school education appear to be in the country illegally (Passel and Cohn 2009a), suggesting that the majority of the least-skilled immigrants are unauthorized. Relative to similarly skilled natives, low-skilled immigrants have high labor force participation and employment rates (Passel and Cohn 2009a) and low rates of crime participation (Butcher and Piehl 2006).

The United States and the EU have each considered expanding temporary immigration to absorb their illegal immigrant populations (Walmsley and Winters 2005). Large-scale illegal entry in the United States began after the end of the Bracero Program (1942–64), which admitted large numbers of seasonal laborers from Mexico and the Caribbean to work on U.S. farms (Calavita 1992). Could new temporary worker programs end illegal inflows? Unless interior enforcement is highly effective at preventing employers from hiring illegal immigrants, a temporary worker program that rations entry would not curtail the employment of unauthorized laborers. Instead, this approach would simply push these workers deeper into the underground economy (Djajic 1999; Epstein, Hillman, and Weiss 1999).

Summary

The emergence of large-scale illegal immigration in the United States can be understood as the result of a conflict between two conflicting desires: to allow immigration of low-skilled individuals while maintaining a welfare state. The mechanisms that govern illegal immigration select individuals with a strong motivation to work while restricting their access to government benefits. The advantage of such a system is that it subjects immigration to market forces, producing a level of foreign labor inflows and a composition of immigrants that reflect relative economic opportunities in sending and receiving countries. In practice, illegal immigration appears to be more flexible and more responsive to economic conditions than legal immigration (Hanson 2007).

Yet, clear disadvantages to illegal immigration exist. Illegal immigration creates a class of individuals with poorly defined residency rights, who, in the absence of occasional amnesties, lack a defined path to citizenship. The presence of a large population of individuals without official resident status implicitly undermines civil society in the United States by weakening democratic norms and reducing the incentive of politicians to respond to the needs of their constituents (Huntington 2004). The challenge for policymakers is to design an immigration regime that has the appealing efficiency properties of illegal immigration—in terms of its flexibility, screening mechanisms, and relatively low fiscal cost—but lacks its negative consequences—the undermining of U.S. law and civil society and the lack of many protections for immigrants.

2

Policy Options for Regulating
Low-Skilled Immigration

Two strategies for regulating illegal immigration are common in immigration reform debate. The first is to prevent illegal entry through increased border enforcement and more assiduous monitoring of worksites in the interior. This strategy, pursued on its own, would lower total U.S. immigration by reducing the size of the undocumented population. During the mid-2000s, net immigration added an average of 1.5 million individuals per year to the United States; approximately half a million of these were unauthorized (Passel and Cohn 2009a). These data suggest that an enforcement strategy focused on reducing illegal immigration through border and workplace enforcement would likely reduce total annual immigration inflows by about a third.

The second strategy is to convert illegal immigrants into legal immigrants by expanding options for legal entry. Net immigration would remain similar to current levels, but illegal immigration would decrease as the existing undocumented population became legalized, and future low-skilled immigrants were offered new channels for legal admission, most likely through a temporary or provisional work visa program. Both strategies reduce illegal immigration, but each has a different effect on the overall *level* of immigration. An enforcement strategy reduces overall entry, while a legalization strategy keeps it high. (Congress, with its proclivity for compromise, has devoted most of its attention to legislative proposals that blend legalization and enforcement strategies.) However, focusing solely on the *level* of immigration obscures other aspects of immigration reform that have important implications for national welfare.

The mechanisms the government uses to select low-skilled immigrants for admission determine the composition of incoming workers in terms of their anticipated productivity and attachment to the labor force. Foreign workers who are more productive and motivated generate a larger immigration surplus for the country; the U.S. government can control this immigration surplus by regulating the supply of visas and the demand for labor. Greater flexibility in visa supply weakens government control over immigration levels but increases the productivity gain from foreign labor inflows and reduces the cost of enforcing against illegal immigration. The scope of residency rights the U.S. government extends through its visas is another important consideration, affecting both the fiscal impact of new immigration and immigrants' incentives to assimilate. Here, the United States faces a tradeoff: Narrower rights reduce immigration's fiscal cost but weaken immigrants' incentives to make investments that enhance their contribution to U.S. society.

Using the analytical framework developed in chapter 1, I examine three broad choices the government will need to make concerning the mechanisms that govern immigration:

- Whether to regulate the entry of immigrants using prices or quantities

- How much variance to allow in the number of legal immigration visas

- How to balance the fiscal cost of immigration with incentives for assimilation

The manner in which the U.S. government approaches these choices will play a large role in determining the impact of immigration reform on U.S. productivity, public finances, and the integration of immigrants into society.

Prices versus Quantities

The current regime of illegal immigration is price-regulated, as the intensity of border and interior enforcement affects the "fee" that prospective immigrants must pay to enter the United States. The current regime of temporary low-skilled immigration, embodied in the H-2A and H-2B visa programs, is primarily quantity-regulated, as Congress determines how many admission slots are available each year. Under one possible strategy for reducing illegal immigration, Congress could increase the number of temporary visas available through the H-2A and H-2B programs, thereby absorbing prospective illegal immigrants into the pool of temporary legal immigrants. The immigration reform packages Congress considered in 2007 loosely followed this approach.[1] This kind of quantity-based strategy would change the composition of individuals who enter the country.

Because illegal immigrants pay a "fee" at the border, the current regime tends to attract individuals who expect a sizable increase in income after moving to the United States. To justify the price that they pay to smugglers and the physical risks they incur in crossing the border, migrants must expect to earn enough to compensate for their significant upfront investments. As I discussed in chapter 1, a price mechanism selects illegal immigrants who have relatively high motivation to be productive workers. Since worker education is an indicator of worker productivity, the average education level of illegal immigrants tends to rise when the United States increases the level of border enforcement (Orrenius and Zavodny 2005).

A price-based selection mechanism also helps U.S. employers solve the problem of finding desirable low-skilled workers. Individuals with low levels of education and little or no U.S. work experience are difficult for U.S. employers to evaluate in terms of productivity. How do businesses determine which prospective employees are likely to work hard, learn quickly on the job, and show up to work on time? Existing immigrant employees are an important source of information about potential hires (Massey, Goldring, and Durand 1994; Munshi 2003), but such networks are imperfect, as they are typically bound by the limits of community or kinship. An entry fee screens out individuals whose expected gain in productivity from migration is low, providing employers with a pool of relatively able and motivated low-skilled workers.

If Congress chooses to increase quantity-based regulation of low-skilled temporary immigration, the U.S. economy will lose many of the desirable incentive properties of the current illegal immigration system, unless employers find a way to select more productive workers from the pool of those seeking temporary visas. Quantity-based entry regulation will also affect the composition of incoming workers by favoring immigrants from traditional sending regions and countries, as employers will have better access to information about prospective temporary workers through established migration networks. Prospective immigrants without access to these networks will be at a disadvantage.

One desirable alternative to enlarging the H-2A and H-2B programs is to allocate temporary work visas through a price mechanism. This allocation can be accomplished either by charging significant processing fees to visa applicants or by auctioning visas outright (Freeman 2006). One frequent objection to auctioning visas is the perception that doing so amounts to putting U.S. citizenship up for sale (North 2010). However, under the current illegal immigration regime, the country effectively "sells" residency rights by controlling the entry fee for immigrants. Establishing entry prices to regulate low-skilled legal immigration would not fundamentally alter the mechanism that currently governs illegal immigration.

What *would* change is that the U.S. government, rather than the *coyotes,* would collect entry fees. Accordingly, immigrants would be subject to less uncertainty regarding their residency rights and face less risk of abuse or physical harm when entering the country. Given that illegal immigrants from Mexico currently pay an average of $2,000 to smugglers to enter the United States illegally (Borger 2009), one would expect that the price individuals would be willing to pay for *legal* admission would be much higher. Immigrants holding visas would have well defined residency rights in the United States and face no risk of deportation while the visa remained valid.

Under this system, the U.S. government would benefit fiscally as immigrants benefited from an improved quality of life. With gross inflows of illegal immigrants from Mexico exceeding 600,000 per year during the mid-2000s (Passel and Cohn 2009b), and assuming an average entry fee of $2,000, the United States has effectively bypassed the opportunity to collect revenues of at least $1.2 billion a year from undocumented migrants. To put this figure in perspective, $1.2 billion a year is equal to 21 percent of the total federal revenues generated by immigration and custom fees in fiscal year 2008.[2]

Flexibility versus Control

Rigid quantity limits are a longstanding feature of U.S. policy on legal immigration. For permanent residents, the Immigration Act of 1990 set an overall annual cap on the number of green cards at 675,000, with specific quotas assigned to immigrants who are family-sponsored (480,000), employment-based (140,000), or entering by lottery (55,000) (U.S. Department of Homeland Security 2009). Immediate relatives of U.S. citizens enter without restriction, while refugees and asylees have their own visa category. Temporary workers enter under an alphabet soup of visa programs, though the scope of these programs is generally small. The largest are the H-1B program for skilled workers, the H-2B program for seasonal non-agricultural workers, and the H-2A program for seasonal agricultural workers. No other temporary visa program admits significant numbers of low-skilled workers. Congress occasionally adjusts visa levels, as it did for H-1Bs at the height of the technology boom in the late 1990s, but, in general, the number of temporary visas made available is unresponsive to market conditions.

The proposals for immigration reform that Congress considered in 2007 were roundly criticized for maintaining an emphasis on rigid visa caps.[3] Rigidity gives Congress control over the *level* of legal immigration, a policy feature that opponents of open immigration tend to favor. However, this rigidity has a high economic cost. In the U.S. economy, wages for low-skilled labor rise and fall over the business cycle, reflecting changes in the productivity of labor (Abraham and Haltiwanger 1995). Wages peak during booms, as rising demand for goods and services pushes prices up, which translates into each worker generating more revenue per hour worked. Correspondingly, wages trough during recessions, as falling demand lets prices drop, bringing wages down, too. The value to U.S. business of having access to low-skilled labor is greatest when GDP growth is high, and least when it is low. Caps on temporary worker visas are not sensitive to these variations in the business cycle.

Rather than keeping immigration levels constant over time, the U.S. economy would benefit from increasing immigration levels during times of economic expansion, and decreasing levels during times of contraction. Even if Congress retained a multiyear cap on immigration levels, the U.S. economy would benefit from a system that allowed the number of visas to fluctuate annually, thereby maximizing the productive contribution of foreign labor. The current regime of illegal immigration accomplishes such adjustments endogenously, as the supply of illegal immigrants responds to market signals (Hanson and Spilimbergo 1999; Passel and Cohn 2009b).

Illegal immigration surges when the U.S. economy grows (or Mexico's economy shrinks) and vice versa.

Another benefit of making legal immigration responsive to the business cycle is that it would help contain the cost of enforcement against illegal immigration. As the level of illegal immigration varies according to the business cycle, so too does the cost of enforcement against illegal immigration. Suppose, for instance, that the government wished to keep growth of the illegal immigrant population below 100,000 individuals per year, which is roughly one-fifth the pre–2007 recession level. During a period of high U.S. GDP growth, the number of migrants attempting to enter the country illegally would increase and, unless the number of legal immigration visas also increased, the Department of Homeland Security would have to devote more resources to enforcement to achieve the 100,000-entrant goal. Conversely, during a period of low GDP growth, DHS would be able to spend less on enforcement and still reach that goal. A flexible visa policy would eliminate the need to increase enforcement spending during economic booms, which, in turn, would help to contain the total cost of managing the immigration system.

Regulating entry of low-skilled immigrants through a price mechanism and making the supply of visas responsive to economic conditions are complementary policies. Suppose the United States were to set a target price for a low-skilled immigration visa that would allow an individual to work in the country for a period of two years. A not-unreasonable figure for this visa is $10,000, which is roughly half of the two-year gain in income that the typical worker from Mexico would reap by migrating to the United States (Hanson 2009). If visas were allocated through periodic auctions, the government could vary the supply in order to keep the market clearing price close to the $10,000 target. During times of rapid economic growth, wage offers from employers would rise, increasing demand for visas and pushing up their price. The government would receive a signal to increase the visa supply in order to keep prices stable. As the economy cooled off, demand for visas would fall, and the government would reduce the supply accordingly. This flexible, price-regulated system is inherently different from the existing H-2A and H-2B programs, which generate minimal revenue for the United States and allocate visas according to fixed criteria.

Fiscal Exposure versus the Incentive to Assimilate

For the U.S. taxpayer, one attractive reason *not* to expand legal entry options for low-skilled immigrants is that illegal entry mitigates the fiscal cost of admitting foreign workers. Non-citizens in the United States are ineligible for most federally funded entitlement programs. As a consequence, even though most families headed by illegal immigrants earn very low incomes, they make minimal use of means-tested cash welfare programs, energy assistance programs, or housing subsidies (Camarota 2004). Although immigrants holding green cards are eligible for these benefits after five years of residence (at which point they can naturalize), illegal immigrants have no such option. Undocumented immigrants do draw on public expenditure in other ways, especially through their children, who are eligible to attend public schools and, if born in the United States, to receive Medicaid and participate in school breakfast and lunch programs. Illegal immigrants generally pay less in taxes than they absorb in public services; by one estimate, the net fiscal cost per immigrant household totals $2,700 (Camarota 2004).

If a reform policy that legalized current illegal immigrants also provided a path to citizenship, such a policy would ultimately increase the fiscal burden on U.S. taxpayers. As citizens, low-skilled immigrants would receive many benefits currently denied to them, but, given their low incomes, they would not pay enough in taxes to balance the cost of these benefits.

Yet, a legalization strategy would also benefit the United States in important ways. After an individual attains legal permanent residence, he has a stronger incentive to make investments in U.S. society, such as seeking education in skills relevant to his U.S. occupation, purchasing a home, joining a local church, and volunteering in the community. Stronger investment incentives mean higher productivity (Kossoudji and Cobb-Clark 2002), greater earnings potential, and an enhanced capacity to contribute to society.

One method of balancing the reduced fiscal exposure of illegal immigration with the productive investment incentives of legal immigration is to offer low-skilled legal immigrants a graduated sequence of residency rights. An initial entry visa would authorize immigrants to work in the country for a defined period of time but would not allow them to bring family members into the country or to receive government benefits beyond an employer-sponsored health care plan. These initial visas could be enforced relatively easily by requiring entrants to post a bond that would be returned to them upon exiting the country at the end of their work period. Compliance with regulations would make immigrants eligible to renew their visas and, after a specified number of renewals, to obtain additional residency rights, including the right to bring family members into the country, and, ultimately, the right to apply for legal permanent residence. Under a graduated system of this kind, an immigrant's initial provisional status would reduce the cost to the U.S. taxpayer, and the well defined path to legal permanent residence would create desirable investment incentives.

A system of graduated residency rights would complement the flexible price mechanism I proposed earlier in this chapter. If immigrants were to purchase a sequence of provisional work visas, they would contribute to U.S. tax revenues in advance of bringing their family members into the country. The upfront expense of obtaining a visa (whether paid for by immigrants or employers) would function as a "down payment" on the public services that the immigrant and his family would ultimately receive. In contrast to the current regime of illegal immigration, in which immigrants have only a vague hope for legalization at some distant point in the future (through amnesty), the process of graduated residency rights fosters immigrants' hopes for permanent residency while providing them with immediate opportunities to contribute to the U.S. economy.

3

Conclusion and Recommendations for Congress

The public debate over immigration reform in 2006 and 2007 was divisive and bitter. The next attempt at an overhaul, which may begin in 2010, promises to be no less discordant. The good news is that the annual net impact of illegal immigration on the U.S. economy, at least in the short run, does not appear to be very large. Although some critics claim that a high level of low-skilled immigration represents a grave danger to America (for example, Huntington 2004), the economics do not support such an argument. Still, there is immense room for improvement in the government's management of foreign labor inflows. Done poorly, immigration reform could, without a doubt, leave the country worse off. In concluding my discussion of regulating low-skilled immigration, I begin by examining estimates of the overall impact of illegal immigration on the U.S. economy. Then, I outline a set of principles for Congress to follow as it considers reform proposals for managing foreign labor inflows.

The Impact of Immigration on the U.S. Economy

Economic theory identifies three ways in which immigration affects the U.S. economy (Borjas 1999). The increase in the supply of labor tends to put downward pressure on wages, redistributing income from workers to employers. Beyond the income gain from lower labor costs, employers also benefit by being able to utilize their land, capital, and technology more productively. The first effect leaves U.S. GDP unchanged, as the fall in workers' income is offset by the rise in employers' income. The second effect yields an immigration surplus, which represents a net increase in national income. The size of the surplus depends on the productive potential of the arriving labor. In 2008, illegal immigrants accounted for approximately 5.7 percent of the U.S. labor force.[1] Using standard economic methods, I calculate that the surplus from illegal immigration is on the order of 0.03 percent of U.S. GDP (Hanson 2007).[2]

The third effect from immigration is a change in the net tax burden on U.S. households, equal to the difference between immigrant demands on government services and immigrant contributions to tax revenues. Whether the tax burden rises or falls depends on how much income immigrants earn, the size and structure of their families, and whether they receive public benefits. Based on the profile of immigrant households in the U.S. Current Population Survey, households headed by an illegal immigrant appear to generate a short-run net fiscal cost on the order of 0.1 percent of U.S. GDP (Camarota 2004; Hanson 2007).[3] Adding the small positive immigration surplus to the small negative net fiscal impact, the total change in U.S. GDP from illegal immigration is a negligible –0.07 percent of GDP.

There are obviously many caveats in producing such estimates. Yet, even with changes in assumptions underlying the economic models used to calculate the immigration surplus, it would be difficult to alter the estimated impact of immigration on the U.S. economy by an order of magnitude in either direction. The size of the labor inflow represented by illegal immigrants is simply not large enough to have a major effect on U.S. GDP. However, illegal immigration has enormous economic ramifications for the immigrants themselves. For illegal immigrants from Mexico, who account for 59 percent of the total undocumented population, the gain in labor income from moving to the United States is equivalent to approximately 1.2 percent of U.S. GDP (Hanson 2009).[4] Since this gain accrues to immigrants, it receives little weight in U.S. policy decisions.

Although the United States does not have a large share of its GDP riding on the outcome of the debate over illegal immigration, Congress will ultimately make decisions that raise or lower the impact of low-skilled foreign labor on the U.S. economy. In chapter 2, I make the case that the United States could maximize the overall gain from immigration by increasing the skill level of immigrants and decreasing the net fiscal costs they generate. Does this mean that the country would be better off shutting down low-skilled immigration and shifting legal immigration toward skilled workers? Surprisingly, perhaps, the answer is no.

Restricting the immigration of low-skilled workers would require eliminating the entry of undocumented workers—in itself an expensive process. The combined budgets of Customs and Border Protection and Immigration and Customs Enforcement, the two Department of Homeland Security agencies that oversee border and interior enforcement, are currently $15 billion, or 0.1 percent of U.S. GDP. Under existing enforcement spending, the population of undocumented immigrants is growing by an average of 500,000 individuals per year. For the sake of argument, suppose that doubling the enforcement budget would reduce the population of illegal immigrants by half, which (if anything) overstates the effects of greater enforcement spending. The result would actually be a net *loss* in U.S. GDP. Spending would increase by 0.1 percent of GDP, but the net impact of immigration on the U.S. economy would only change by 0.035 percent of GDP (0.5 x 0.07 percent). Thus, the overall U.S. national income would decline by approximately -0.065 percent. The calculus would change, of course, if the government found a way to make existing enforcement spending more effective at reducing illegal entry. But that is a big "if." One would need to be quite optimistic about the effectiveness of future enforcement for a pure enforcement strategy to be cost-effective.

As an alternative, Congress should consider visa programs that could raise the net gain from immigration by making low-skilled immigrants more productive and reducing the fiscal exposure to taxpayers. Rather than endorsing a particular scheme, I will summarize the broad precepts that Congress should follow in designing a new system that expands the economic benefits from immigration. To enact successful reform, the government should abide by three principles in its management of low-skilled immigration.

First Principle:
Use a Price Mechanism to Allocate Temporary Work Visas

Because policies designed to keep low-skilled workers out of the United States are costly and ineffective, the government should focus on ensuring that low-skilled immigrants are as productive as possible and generate as much tax revenue as possible. Requiring that low-skilled immigrants pay an entry fee to obtain a visa would attract individuals who foresee a relatively high gain in their productivity from migrating; these are the low-skilled workers likely to make the largest contribution to the U.S. economy. Entry fees would also generate revenue for the U.S. government, which would off-set the cost of managing the immigration system and balance the indirect fiscal consequences associated with providing public services to an increased low-skilled immigrant population.

Suppose, for instance, that the U.S. government determined how many visas to make available and then auctioned these visas on the open market, with the auction price determining the entry fee. An entry fee would effec-tively "tax" the hiring of low-skilled immigrants. Economic theory suggests that it does not matter much in terms of the economic consequences whether such a tax is levied on the employers who wish to hire immigrant labor or on the immigrants themselves. Who actually bears the tax depends in large part on the elasticity of supply for foreign labor. With U.S. wages far exceed-ing wages in Mexico and Central America (which together account for 70 percent of the unauthorized immigrants in the United States [Passel and Cohn 2009a]), there will always be enough demand to sell the available sup-ply of visas. Because the visa supply would restrict the number of entrants, the supply of foreign workers would be inelastic, and the "tax" would be borne primarily by immigrants. Thus, even if the entry tax were levied on employers (as would occur if employers were required to purchase the right to hire foreign workers through a visa auction), immigrants would end up bearing its cost. The entry tax would lower employer demand for foreign workers, leading to a reduction in immigrant wages, and thereby indirectly compensating employers for expenses incurred in acquiring visa rights.

Even if a price mechanism resulted in lower real wages (i.e., net of the entry tax) for immigrants in the United States, there would still be a large number of prospective immigrants desiring to enter the country. The inelas-ticity of foreign labor supply means that, no matter whether an entry fee is levied on immigrants or paid for by employers, foreign labor ultimately bears the cost. It is important to keep in mind that illegal immigrants already bear a tax of sorts in the entry fees they pay to smugglers. Therefore, under a price mechanism, immigrants would not necessarily face an increased entry fee; rather, they would substitute the cost of a visa for the cost of a smuggler. And immigrants would get more for their money—a fee paid to the U.S. government would yield residency rights and benefits currently denied to illegal immigrants. Low-skilled immigrants would be freed from the risks of crossing the border illegally and relieved of the threat of deportation once resident in the United States.

Second Principle:
Allow the Supply of Visas to Fluctuate with the Business Cycle

The immigration surplus that low-skilled workers generate will be larger if the supply of visas is made responsive to economic conditions. The gain to U.S. employers from hiring foreign labor rises during economic expansions and falls during economic contractions. For any given level of immigration, increasing the supply of visas during booms and decreasing it during busts would raise the productivity gain to the U.S. economy from foreign labor inflows.

Another benefit of variable visa supply is that it would reduce the cost of enforcing against illegal immigration. As long as the United States regulates entry at its borders, some immigrants will attempt to enter the country illegally, requiring the maintenance of an enforcement presence. Flexibility in visa supply would help contain the cost of this enforcement by expanding options for legal entry when attempted illegal immigration would otherwise be at its peak.

Third Principle:
Require Immigrants to Earn Long-Term Residency Rights

Entry fees and variable visa supplies resolve the problem of how to manage the inflow of immigrants on a day-to-day basis. However, they do not address the long-run issue of whether the United States is better off maintaining a temporary status for low-skilled immigrants or allowing them to become permanent residents. The choice is not an easy one. Maintaining temporary status for foreign labor inflows contains the fiscal obligations from immigration but requires a significant enforcement infrastructure to ensure that workers return home after their visas expire. Admitting foreign labor as permanent residents gives immigrants strong incentives to contribute to U.S. society but also exposes U.S. taxpayers to myriad fiscal costs.

Immigrants themselves also may be conflicted about the choice between temporary and permanent status. Some may view temporary residence in the United States as a means to earn the extra income they need to pursue their long-term life goals elsewhere. Others may be intent on becoming U.S. citizens. A system that requires all immigrants to be temporary does not accommodate such heterogeneity.

It is possible to avoid both the enforcement costs associated with temporary immigration and the fiscal exposure associated with permanent residence by offering immigrants the option of earning the right to stay in the United States for progressively longer periods of time. The hurdle for obtaining an initial, temporary visa should be set relatively low, amounting to not much more than paying an entry fee and securing a job with a U.S. employer. Subsequent visas would offer broader residency rights and the option to bring family members into the country; ultimately, obtaining permanent residence would require an immigrant to accumulate a multiyear record of having abided by all pertinent rules and regulations. This graduated system of residency rights would provide strong incentives to abide by immigration law. Immigrants would gain by having a well defined path to citizenship, if not an easy one. They would also benefit from being able to choose from various options regarding their work presence in the United States.

Summary

When Congress next chooses to address immigration reform, it should seek first to do no harm. The current regime of illegal immigration, imperfect as it is, is market-tested. Despite the hyperbole from various quarters, it has not done significant harm to the U.S. economy. The current regime has many positive elements that would be lost if the country chose to increase existing temporary worker programs, as many have advocated. An enforcement strategy alone, which also has many adherents, fails a basic cost-benefit test. Constructive reform requires allowing low-skilled immigration to occur under a legal framework that respects market mechanisms and treats immigrants as individuals with the potential to contribute to U.S. society. Unless Congress recognizes and understands the successes and failures of low-skilled immigration policy to date, we risk losing another chance to get reform right.

Notes

Introduction

1. While President Obama initially suggested he would address immigration reform early in his tenure, he has put it off until late in 2010 at the earliest. See Ginger Thompson and Marc Lacey, "Obama Says Immigration Changes Remain on His Agenda but for 2010 Enactment," *New York Times,* August 11, 2009, A6.

2. See http://www.dhs.gov/ximgtn/statistics/.

3. This estimate is based on the number of working-age illegal immigrants with less than a high school education reported in Passel and Cohn (2009a).

4. Much is made of the fact that unauthorized immigrants are breaking the law. However, in many respects, these individuals are well integrated into U.S. society. Illegal immigrants work in established businesses, own their own homes, shop in neighborhood stores, attend local churches, and send their children to public schools. Like legal residents, they sometimes default on their mortgages. Many have payroll taxes deducted from their paychecks, and a smaller but still significant number pay federal income taxes (Camarota 2004). Until the Department of Homeland Security enacted stricter interior enforcement policies in 2006, illegal immigrants' presence in the country was unofficially tolerated.

5. Crossing the U.S.–Mexico border, the method of entry for 60 to 70 percent of illegal entrants, is perilous, resulting in hundreds of deaths each year (Cornelius and Salehyan 2007). A two-decade-long expansion in the size and scope of the U.S. Border Patrol has given the agency significant enforcement capability. Evading capture by the Border Patrol entails physical risks and is expensive; the price for border smuggler (*coyote*) services averaged $2,000 in 2008 (Borger 2009). This "entry fee" is part of the cost of joining the U.S. labor force.

6. Over the period between 1999 and 2008, 44 percent of new legal permanent residence visas issued by the U.S. government went to immediate family members of U.S. citizens, 21 percent to other family members, and 15 percent to immigrants sponsored by their employers. Most of the remaining share was issued to refugees or asylees or individuals obtaining a green card through a lottery (the diversity program). See U.S. Department of Homeland Security (2009).

7. Several recent contributions provide excellent discussions of the specific policy instruments the United States currently uses to manage immigration and practical guides for refining or redesigning these instruments to better serve U.S. economic interests. See: Spencer Abraham and Lee H. Hamilton, "Immigration and America's Future: A New Chapter," Migration Policy Institute, 2006; Jeb Bush, Thomas F. McLarty III, and Edward Alden, "U.S. Immigration Policy," Council on Foreign Relations, Independent Task Force Report No. 63, 2009; and Pia Orrenius and Madeline Zavodny, *Beside the Golden Door: U.S. Immigration Reform in a New Era of Globalization*, American Enterprise Institute, 2010.

Chapter 1

1. See Miriam Jordan, "As Border Tightens, Growers See Threat to 'Winter Salad Bowl,'" *Wall Street Journal*, March 11, 2005, 1.

2. See Mark Krikorian, "Lured by Jobs, Illegal Immigrants Risk Death at Border Crossings," *Santa Barbara News-Press*, April 25, 1999.

3. See Tunku Varadarajan, "The Romance of Economics," *Wall Street Journal*, July 22, 2006.

4. Under the current U.S. Department of Labor labor certification process, employers must certify that U.S. workers are not available to perform a job before they can hire a nonimmigrant worker. They must also certify that the wages and working conditions meet regional standards (U.S. Department of Homeland Security 2009).

5. In the European Union, these inflows do not translate into large stocks of illegal immigrants, because European countries tend to offer frequent amnesties to unauthorized immigrants. Greece, Italy, Portugal, and Spain have each offered multiple amnesties in the last decade, which has kept the share of illegals in the region's foreign-born population under 10 percent (Maas 2009).

6. See U.S. Office of Management and Budget 2009.

7. CBP and ICE are agencies with the U.S. Department for Homeland Security. See U.S. Office of Management and Budget 2009.

8. Individuals with H-1B visas may extend their stay beyond six years if they have an application for legal permanent residence that is pending.

9. In the case of *United States v. Wong Kim Ark* (1898), the Supreme Court ruled that children born to permanent immigrants were U.S. citizens. The case dealt with legal immigrants. While the Supreme Court has never ruled on whether children of illegal immigrants are U.S. citizens, the presumption is that they are (Meese, Forte, Spalding 2005).

Chapter 2

1. See Orrenius and Zavodny (2010).

2. See U.S. Office of Management and Budget (2009).

3. See Bush, MacLarty, and Alden (2009) and Orrenius and Zavodny (2010).

Chapter 3

1. The figure comes from the Passel and Cohn (2009a) estimate that in 2008 there were 8.3 million unauthorized immigrants employed in the United States and the Bureau of Labor Statistics figure that in 2008 the average civilian employment was 145.7 million.

2. From Borjas (1999), the formula for the immigration surplus is: 0.5 × labor's share of national income × wage elasticity × immigrant share of the labor force. Labor's share of national income is approximately 0.7. The wage elasticity is the percent change in wages from a 1 percent increase in labor supply due to immigration, which I take to be 0.3, as reported in Borjas (2003). Note that if one thinks the impact of immigration on wages is smaller than Borjas's (2003) estimates, the estimated surplus from immigration is correspondingly reduced.

3. "Short" means that future taxes and spending associated with immigrants and their descendents are ignored. See Smith and Edmonston (1997) and Borjas (1999) for a discussion.

4. This figure does not include any income gains with fiscal transfers that illegal immigrant households receive from the U.S. government.

References

Abraham, Katherine, and John Haltiwanger. 1995. Real Wages over the Business Cycle. *Journal of Economic Literature* 33 (September): 1216–64.

Abraham, Spencer, and Lee H. Hamilton. 2006. Immigration and America's Future: A New Chapter. Migration Policy Institute.

Bertocchi, Graziella, and Chiara Strozzi. 2006. The Evolution of Citizenship: Economic and Institutional Determinants. IZA Discussion Paper No. 2510.

Borger, Scott. 2009. Essays on Migration and Monetary Policy. Ph.D. diss., Department of Economics, University of California, San Diego.

Borjas, George J. 1999. *Heaven's Door: Immigration Policy and the American Economy.* Princeton, N.J.: Princeton University Press.

———. 2003. The Labor Demand Curve Is Downward Sloping: Reexamining the Impact of Immigration on the Labor Market. *Quarterly Journal of Economics* 118 (November): 1335–74.

Briggs, Vernon. 2001. *Immigration and American Unionism.* Ithaca, N.Y.: Cornell University Press.

———. 2004. Guestworker Programs: Lessons from the Past and Warnings for the Future. Center for Immigration Studies.

Bush, Jeb, Thomas F. McLarty III, and Edward Alden. 2009. U.S. Immigration Policy. Council on Foreign Relations, Independent Task Force Report No. 63.

Butcher, Kristin, and Anne Morrison Piehl. 2006. Why are Immigrants' Incarceration Rates So Low? Evidence on Selective Immigration, Deterrence, and Deportation. Mimeo, Wellesley College.

Calavita, Kitty. 1992. *Inside the State: The Bracero Program, Immigration, and the I.N.S.* New York: Routledge.

Camarota, Steven A. 2004. The High Cost of Cheap Labor: Illegal Immigration and the Federal Budget. Center for Immigration Studies.

———. 2005. Immigration at Mid Decade: A Snapshot of America's Foreign Born Population in 2005. Center for Immigration Studies.

———. 2008. Homeward Bound: Recent Immigration Enforcement and the Decline in the Illegal Alien Population. Center for Immigration Studies.

Card, David. 2005. Is the New Immigration Really So Bad? *Economic Journal* 115, no. 507:300–23.

Clemons, Michael, Claudio Montenegro, and Lant Pritchett. 2008. The Great Discrimination: Borders as a Labor Market Barrier. Mimeo, Center on Global Development.

Cornelius, Wayne, A., and Ideal Salehyan. 2007. Does Border Enforcement Deter Unauthorized Immigration?—The Case of Mexican Migration to the United States. *Regulation & Governance* 1, no. 2 (June): 139–53.

Cortes, Patricia. 2008. The Effect of Low-Skilled Immigration on U.S. Prices: Evidence from CPI Data. *Journal of Political Economy* 116, no. 3:381–422.

Cox, Adam B., and Eric A. Posner. 2007. The Second Order Structure of U.S. Immigration Law. *Stanford Law Review* 59: 809.

Djajic, Slobodan. 1999. Dynamics of Immigration Control. *Journal of Population Economics* 12, no. 1:45–61.

Epstein, Gil S., Arye L. Hillman, and Avi Weiss. 1999. Creating Illegal Immigrants. *Journal of Population Economics* 12:3–21.

Ethier, Wilfred. 1986. Illegal Immigration: The Host-Country Problem. *American Economic Review* 76, no. 1 (March): 56–71.

Facchini, Giovanni, Anna Maria Mayda, and Prachi Mishra. 2008. Do Interest Groups Affect Immigration? Mimeo, Georgetown University.

Fix, Michael, and Jeffrey Passel. 2002. The Scope and Impact of Welfare Reform's Immigrant Provisions. Washington, D.C.: The Urban Institute.

Freeman, Richard B. 2006. People Flows in Globalization. *Journal of Economic Perspectives* 20, no. 2 (Spring): 145–70.

Gathmann, Christina. 2008. Effects of Enforcement on Illegal Markets: Evidence from Migrant Smuggling on the Southwestern Border. *Journal of Public Economics* 92, no. 10-11:1926–41.

Hanson, Gordon H. 2005. Why Does Immigration Divide America? Public Finance and Political Opposition to Open Borders. Washington, D.C.: Institute for International Economics.

———. 2006. Illegal Migration from Mexico to the United States. *Journal of Economic Literature* 44:869–924.

———. 2007. The Economic Logic of Illegal Immigration. Council Special Report No. 26, Council on Foreign Relations.

———. 2009. The Economic Consequences of the International Migration of Labor. *Annual Review of Economics.*

———. 2010. International Migration and the Developing World. In Dani Rodrik and Mark Rosenzweig, eds., *Handbook of Development Economics.* Amsterdam: North Holland.

Hanson, Gordon H., Kenneth Scheve, and Matthew J. Slaughter. 2007. Local Public Finance and Individual Preferences over Globalization Strategies. *Economics and Politics* 19:1–33.

Hanson, Gordon H., and Antonio Spilimbergo. 1999. Illegal Immigration, Border Enforcement and Relative Wages: Evidence from Apprehensions at the U.S.-Mexico Border. *American Economic Review* 89:1337–57.

———. 2001. Political Economy, Sectoral Shocks, and Border Enforcement, *Canadian Journal of Economics* 34:612–38.

Huntington, Samuel. 2004. *Who Are We? The Challenges to America's National Identity.* New York: Simon and Schuster.

Jandl, Michael. 2003. Estimates on the Number of Illegal and Smuggled Immigrants in Europe. International Centre for Migration Policy Development.

Jordan, Mirian. 2005. As Border Tightens, Growers See Threat to "Winter Salad Bowl." *Wall Street Journal,* March 11, 1.

Kossoudji, Sherrie A., and Cobb-Clark, Deborah A. 2002. Coming Out of the Shadows: Learning about Legal Status and Wages from the Legalized Population. *Journal of Labor Economics* 20, no. 3:598–628.

Krikorian, Mark, 1999. Lured by Jobs, Illegal Immigrants Risk Death at Border Crossings. *Santa Barbara News-Press,* April 25.

Maas, Willem. 2009. Unauthorized Migration and the Politics of Legalization, Regularization, and Amnesty in Europe. Paper presented at the WPSA Annual Meeting, Vancouver, BC, "Ideas, Interests and Institutions."

Martin, Phillip. 2001. There Is Nothing More Permanent Than Temporary Foreign Workers. Center for Immigration Studies.

Massey, Douglas S. 2004. International Migration at the Dawn of the Twenty-First Century: The Role of the State. *Population and Development Review* 25, no. 2:303–22.

Massey, Douglas S., L. Goldring, and Jorge Durand. 1994. Continuities in Transnational Migration: An Analysis of Nineteen Mexican Communities. *American Journal of Sociology* 99, no. 6:1492–1533.

Mazzolari, Francesca. 2009. Determinants and Effects of Naturalization: Effects of Dual Citizenship Laws. *Demography.*

Meese, Edwin, David F. Forte, and Matthew Spalding. 2005. *The Heritage Guide to the Constitution.* Washington, D.C.: Regnery Publishing.

Munshi, Kaivan. 2003. Networks in the Modern Economy: Mexican Migrants in the U.S. Labor Market. *Quarterly Journal of Economics* 118 (May): 549–97.

North, David. 2010. Green Cards for Rich Family Actually Cost Less Than Previously Reprorted. Center for Immigration Studies, January 13.

Organisation for Economic Co-operation and Development. 2008. *International Migration Outlook.* Paris.

Orrenius, Pia M., and Madeline Zavodny. 2005. Self-Selection among Undocumented Immigrants from Mexico. *Journal of Development Economics* 78, no. 1 (October): 215–40.

———. 2010. *Beside the Golden Door: Immigration Reform in a New Era of Globalization.* Washington, D.C.: AEI Press.

Passel, Jeffrey S., and D'Vera Cohn. 2009a. A Portrait of Unauthorized Immigrants in the United States. Pew Hispanic Center.

———. 2009b. Mexican Immigrants: How Many Come? How Many Leave? Pew Hispanic Center.

Rupert, Elizabeth. 1999. Managing Foreign Labor in Singapore and Malaysia: Are There Lessons for GCC Countries? The World Bank, Policy Research Working Paper Series: 2053.

Scheve, Kenneth F., and Matthew J. Slaughter. 2001. *Globalization and the Perceptions of American Workers.* Washington, D.C.: Institute for International Economics.

Shah, Nasra. 2006. Restrictive Labour Immigration Policies in the Oil Rich Gulf. UN Population Division.

Smith, James P., and Barry Edmonston, eds. 1997. *The New Americans: Economic, Demographic, and Fiscal Effects of Immigration.* Washington, D.C.: National Academy Press.

Thompson, Ginger, and Marc Lacey. 2009. Obama Says Immigration Changes Remain on His Agenda but for 2010 Enactment. *New York Times,* August 11, A6.

U.S. Department of Homeland Security. 2009. *Yearbook of Immigration Statistics.* http://www.dhs.gov/ximgtn/statistics/publications/yearbook.shtm.

U.S. Office of Management and Budget. 2009. *Budget of the United States Government, Fiscal Year 2009.* Washington, D.C.: Government Printing Office.

Varadarajan, Tunku. 2006. The Romance of Economics. *Wall Street Journal,* July 22.

Walmsley, Terrie L., and L. Alan Winters. 2005. Relaxing the Restrictions on the Temporary Movement of Natural Persons: A Simulation Analysis. *Journal of Economic Integration* 20, no. 4:688–726.

Winckler, Onn. 1999. The Immigration Policy of the Gulf Cooperation Council (GCC) States. In Tim Niblock and Rodney Wilson, eds., *The Political Economy of the Middle East.* Northampton, MA: Elgar Reference Collection.

About the Author

Gordon H. Hanson is the director of the Center on Pacific Economies and a professor of economics at the University of California, San Diego (UCSD), where he holds faculty positions in the School of International Relations and Pacific Studies and the Department of Economics. Dr. Hanson is also a research associate at the National Bureau of Economic Research, co-editor of the *Journal of Development Economics,* and a member of the Council on Foreign Relations. Prior to joining UCSD in 2001, he served on the economics faculties of the University of Michigan and the University of Texas. Dr. Hanson has published extensively in top economics journals on issues related to immigration, international trade, and foreign investment.